Camping Is Fun

T0020199

Saving Our Planet

We went camping.

Here is my camera.

I took my camera
with me.

5

Here are the tents.

Here are the chairs.

Here are the beds.

Here are my swimmers.

I took my swimmers
with me.

This is my **fishing rod.** I took my fishing rod with me.

This is my **torch.**

I took my torch

with me.

Camping was fun.

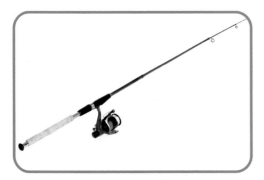

fishing rod

torch